Text
Bill Harris

Captions
Louise Houghton

Design
Teddy Hartshorn

Photography
Black Star
Colour Library Books Ltd
FPG International
New England Stock
Stock Market

Picture Editor
Annette Lerner

Commissioning Editor
Andrew Preston

Publishing Assistant
Edward Doling

Editorial
Jane Adams
Louise Houghton

Production
Ruth Arthur
Sally Connolly
David Proffit
Andrew Whitelaw

Director of Production
Gerald Hughes

Director of Publishing
David Gibbon

CLB 2516
This 1991 edition is published by Crescent Books,
distributed by Outlet Book Company, Inc., a Random House Company,
40 Engelhard Avenue, Avenel, New Jersey 07001.

Random House
New York • Toronto • London • Sydney • Auckland

Printed and bound in Singapore

ISBN 0-517-02542-6

10 9 8 7 6 5

NEW ORLEANS
A PICTURE MEMORY

CRESCENT BOOKS
NEW YORK /AVENEL, NEW JERSEY

It's the least American of all of America's cities. The accent is almost self-consciously French and the most admired architecture has a Spanish flavor. But, though they were late-comers, the Americans put their stamp on New Orleans where it counted most. They cemented its reputation for glamour and set it apart as a place in which to have a good time at a time when other American cities were taking themselves and the idea of respectability very seriously. They called it "Sin City" in the nineteenth century, and most of the people who lived there did everything they could to make sure there was no competition for the honor.

The Americans found fertile ground for wickedness when Louisiana became part of the United States in 1803. The French had been working on it for the better part of ninety years. The Spanish tried to stamp out the debauchery during their thirty-one-year rule, but if they were able to influence the minds of their subjects, they never quite managed to capture their hearts. Most had arrived from France with a completely different dream to that of the immigrants from other parts of Europe who were populating the rest of North America.

The English had been living in Massachusetts for more than a hundred years when a Scotsman named John Law was tossed out of Britain as punishment for his penchant for dueling. He wound up in Paris and charmed his way into the court of Louis XIV, the Sun King himself. Thirty-five years earlier, the French explorer La Salle had sailed down the Mississippi River and claimed the territory around it for his king. Louis was pleased, especially as the new country was named in his honor, and ordered that a city be established at the mouth of the river. The attempt was a disaster, and by the time John Law appeared at Versailles there were fewer than three hundred Frenchmen in Louisiana.

Law looked upon this as a challenge. Promising to increase the population and fill the royal treasury, he secured the right to local pearl fisheries and gold and silver mining and went to work on an advertising campaign to fill the land with people. A pair of Canadian explorers – Pierre Le Moyne (Sieur d'Iberville) and his brother Jean Baptiste Le Moyne (Sieur de Bienville) –

had been exploring Louisiana for twenty years by this time. Even though they had reported that there was no gold or silver to be found and that the pearls were worthless, Law, overlooking this unpromising honesty, appointed Bienville Governor of the colony. It was the only move he made that had any connection with reality. His advertising campaign had warmed the people to the idea of investing in land along the Mississippi. The high-powered salesmen he hired to follow it up established a high-water mark in the history of land speculation. But if the sales pressure separated many a Frenchman from his life's savings, Law's men weren't able to convince many of them to start a new life in Louisiana.

Without colonists, even the most unsophisticated investors knew that there could be no profits. Law solved the problem by offering free land, free transportation and the promise of a life of leisure that could magically produce eternal prosperity. His scheme attracted a few solid citizens, but its greatest appeal was to men they politely called "vagabonds" back in those days. The minions of the King added to the mix by dumping prison inmates and hard-core poverty cases on the new land.

By the time the French began arriving in large numbers, Bienville had established a city on a crescent-shaped bend in the Mississippi River far enough inland to be safe from the storms of the Gulf of Mexico. He called it "Nouvelle-Orléans" in honor of the French Regent, the Duke of Orléans. Thanks to Bienville's dedication, the city grew, but John Law's settlers were almost no help at all. He had promised them a life of ease and they were determined that that promise should be kept. Most flatly refused to work, despite the threat of imminent starvation if the forests weren't cleared and farms established. What Law had created was a welfare state, and the company and the French government both faced bankruptcy supporting it. The problem was solved by the introduction of slavery. In New England, among other places, experiments to enslave the Indians had come to grief. The solution, in the eyes of the French, was to import black Africans. John Law's

Mississippi Company subsidized their sale and offered easy credit to interested buyers – of whom there were plenty. Within twenty years the black population of Louisiana was more than double that of the whites.

By the time Bienville retired in 1743, enough new colonists had been attracted to exactly reverse this proportion and the colony was actually prosperous. But progress took a turn when the government was turned over to the Marquis de Vaudreuil. The new governor established himself and his family and retainers on the banks of the Mississippi on a gaudy scale that rivalled the Court at Versailles. New Orleans was still a frontier town, but the Marquis's balls and entertainments gave it a cosmopolitan atmosphere it retains today. The government was corrupt and attracted the worst kind of people, but if New Orleans was filled with prostitutes and thieves, confidence men and brawlers, it was positively genteel compared to what lay ahead.

The French lost Louisiana to Spain in 1769 and the government fell into the hands of an Irishman named Alexander O'Reilly. He ruled with an iron hand and sent vice underground. In spite of policies that seemed almost repressive by Crescent City standards, the population of Louisiana tripled in the first twenty years of Spanish control and that of New Orleans doubled. The Spanish also enforced an iron rule forbidding Americans to trade on the Mississippi River. If they hadn't lost Louisiana to France again in 1800, the law might have proved to be the salvation of the forces of respectability in New Orleans. In all those years, including the years of almost complete anarchy before the United States bought Louisiana, the citizens of New Orleans, no matter where they stood on the subject of vice, were completely united in their hatred of Americans.

During the years of Spanish rule, the French-speaking settlers began calling themselves "Creoles," and invented the word "Kaintock" to describe all Americans, whether they came from Kentucky or not. Hardly a day went by without someone spreading a rumor that these barbarians were massing up the river to attack the city. Mothers used them to frighten their children into submission and gun dealers found them a better threat than the Indians for boosting sales. Many people thought it was only a matter of time before they'd be forced to defend themselves. When Louisiana became an American possession they had good reason to say "I told you so."

Their fears were probably well-placed. The only Americans most of them had seen were the flatboat crews that had terrorized the city before the Spanish outlawed them. Typically, they were frontiersmen who had found the fontier too tame. But, if hard work is a virtue they could qualify as saints if it weren't for the fact that it was their only virtue. No one in the history of America has ever worked harder. They maneuvered hundred-foot vessels loaded with more than seventy tons of freight over sandbars, through rapids and around fallen trees. Defending themselves against the river pirates who lurked around nearly every bend was no easy job either. The open deck was their bed during the three or four months it took to make the journey from Louisville to New Orleans. The only thing that made life bearable to them was the cask of Monongahela rye whiskey that was a fixture aboard every boat. Without their "old Nongahela," no one would have made the trip, and, in their opinion, few could have survived it. A couple of months of raw whiskey, bad food and all that hard work tended to make a man feisty. By the time the boats docked the men aboard were primed for mayhem. New Orleans was the end of their rainbow. Many shipped down to the city without pay, in fact, just to see if the things people said about New Orleans were true. They were rarely disappointed.

The Americans who arrived in New Orleans in the early years of the nineteenth century were snubbed by the Creoles and forced to live in a ghetto that became known as the Garden District. By the time the barriers came down, the pattern of living was already well-established. The Vieux Carré, the old square, not only never lost its French name, but also managed to escape the kind of civic improvements the Yankees have always had a penchant for.

It must have taken some doing. By the mid-1820s, the population of New Orleans had quadrupled, making Creoles very much an overwhelmed minority. But the newcomers, though nearly all immigrants from other parts of the United States, weren't all cut from the same cloth. It was estimated that about a quarter of them were criminals lured down the river by the city's reputation for wide-open wickedness. About the same percentage were boatmen who had decided to stay. Together they represented a sub-culture of the Americans who were relegated to a section of town where the flatboat crews supported the local economy with their revels. Appropriately enough it was called "the Swamp." Even the police avoided it and Americans and Creoles alike were given to a lot of hand-wringing over whether the Swamp would eventually sink their city. Their salvation arrived from Pittsburgh on January 12, 1812.

It was one of those new-fangled steam boats, built by Robert Fulton himself. The vessel made just three round trips between Crescent City and Natchez before she blew up, but it was more than enough to prove that the Mississippi River and steamboats were made for each other. In less than thirty years there were 450 of them on the river, and not one of them had to steer a berth around a flatboat. Without the flatboat crews, business in the Swamp turned a bit sour, but vice had hardly been run out of town.

The river pirates had also been driven out of business by the bigger, faster vessels, but there were easier ways to turn a dishonest dollar. No steamboat moved in or out of New Orleans without a professional gambler aboard. Every form of gambling ever devised by man was available in the city itself, but there was a special attraction to losing one's money in the gilded saloon of a steamboat. Captains considered it bad luck to leave a wharf without a professional gambler aboard, and their passengers considered it unthinkable. There's no denying they added a touch of class to the voyage.

They rarely had to be pointed out. The only men in America who were better-dressed were probably the gambling passengers themselves. They favored black suits, white shirts with black ties and black high-heeled boots, yet they were far from conservative dressers. Their shirts were embellished with lace and covered by a gaudy bright-colored vest with gold or pearl buttons. They considered themselves undressed without at least three diamond rings, and out of uniform without a diamond stickpin known as a "headlight." They carried a jewel-studded gold pocketwatch attached to a gold chain worn around their neck. The get-up usually advertised them as what were euphemistically known as "sure-thing players." This meant that luck had nothing to do with how they played the game. However, among the people who could afford to pay $30 for a trip up the river to Natchez and another $15 to get back to New Orleans, there were always a few who could prove they were smarter, or at least luckier, than the professional gamblers. But, the deck, as they say, was stacked against them.

The professionals were masters at palming cards and dealing from the bottom of the deck, but they also had technology on their side. Mail order houses kept them supplied with devices for concealing cards up their sleeves, in their belts or in the folds of their vests.

Other paraphernalia included "shiners," tiny mirrors with which to read an opponent's hand, and rings fitted with needles to make indentations on the backs of cards. The sales brochures called them "advantage tools," and they provided the only means of making money from Mississippi River gamblers, who considered them a worthwhile business investment. As one of the catalogues gushed; "The benefits can be estimated in only one way and that is, how much money has your opponent got? For you are certain to get it, whether it is $10 or $10,000; the heavier the stakes the sooner you will break him, and he never knows what hurt him."

The painless extraction continued on a daily basis until the beginning of the Civil War, when leisurely travel on the river became a thing of the past. Most of the gamblers retired to New Orleans, where they formed the "Blackleg Cavalry," dedicated to defending the city from any Yankee invasion. Naturally, they were the best-dressed unit in the Confederate Army, and when they rode out to drill each day hearts swelled with pride. In fact they just rode out of sight and gathered under the trees for friendly games of poker, but they worked wonders for local morale. When the Union Navy finally arrived down the river the Blacklegs rode out to engage them, but turned tail at the sound of gunfire and decided to study war no more. Even though other rebel units stood their ground the Yankees took over New Orleans a few weeks later. But the gamblers had the last laugh. They worked for two years fleecing the conquerors, and by concentrating on quartermasters and paymasters cost the Union Army more dollars than any of its major battles.

The occupying army cut its losses by making gambling illegal, but, as soon as it left, the postwar government began encouraging games of chance and New Orleans became a wide-open town again. While carpetbaggers were flocking to all parts of the South and changing its character, gamblers, gangsters and flim flam men found their way to New Orleans and encouraged a return to its old wicked ways. It took more than twenty years for the city to establish any kind of control over them. During those years New Orleans replaced Sodom and Gomorrah as the favorite theme of fire-breathing preachers all over America. For those who weren't regular church-goers, the Louisiana Lottery served as a drawing card to put New Orleans high on the list of places Americans most wanted to visit. The Lottery, possibly the most successful in the country's history, reached into every corner of the United States and thrived from 1863 until 1907.

Those with the means to make the trip were rarely disappointed. If New Orleans had lived up to the title of "Sin City" in the years before the war, no one disagreed with the sheriff who characterized it as "a perfect hell on earth" in the 1870s.

The city fathers were finally able to cool things down at the turn of the century by confining vice to designated districts. They didn't eliminate it, of course, it was too good for business. But it put respectability back into the picture and that was also good for business. In the process New Orleans blossomed and visitors began to discover what had been there all along – an old-world charm and a zest for life quite unlike anything that existed anywhere else on the American continent. The Creoles may have winked at vice during all those years, and nor were they above participating in it, but it was the Americans who turned it into a circus of depravity. However, most of the old families were convinced that one day the Americans would go away and leave them alone. With that in mind, they doggedly refused to become Americanized, and spent their days in cafés and coffee houses planning for their day of liberation. The day never came, and before long the Americans were joining them at their tables and sharing what they had to offer. They called life in the French Quarter "charming," and if the descendants of the original settlers were clinging to their old traditions as a form of protest, they found more and more newcomers encouraging them. It

is pleasing to report that the charm has survived to this day.

The spice of the life immigrants from America came to admire was provided by jazz music and jazz dancing – still proudly ranked high among the country's unique art forms. When the French began importing black slaves, they also promulgated the "Code Noir," a set of laws designed to prevent the possibility of an uprising. Its restrictions lasted throughout the Spanish occupation, but when the Americans arrived they relaxed some of the rules and began allowing blacks to assemble in specified areas on Sunday afternoons. Eventually the only place the gatherings were allowed was a place that was known as "Congo Square." For decades it was the scene of weekly demonstrations of the dance they called Bamboula, which was a combination of African rhythms and the steps of the French contra-dances. The beat of the jazz music went on far into the night and it can still be heard and felt in all its variations, not just in New Orleans but all over the world. What was born on a Sunday somewhere around 1805 is the city's gift to all of us. But it is only one of many.

The Duke of Orléans was, appropriately, one of the greatest scoundrels in the history of France. As his mother said: "the fairies have given him every gift except a way to make use of them." It's hardly true of his namesake city. They've used their gifts well in New Orleans, and the result is a pure pleasure.

Facing page: Saint Louis Cathedral on Jackson Square.

15

New Orleans' colorful history of European occupation, war, struggle and division has made it a strong and vibrant city. Rising high above the waters of the Mississippi, New Orleans has done a lot of growing since it was established as a seaport in 1718. Downtown New Orleans (these pages and overleaf) is the center for marketing and distribution in the Southern States, though these are no longer carried on in the style of Jean Lafitte, the infamous pirate who operated here in the early nineteenth century.

The deep waters of the Mississippi (these pages and overleaf) can accommodate even the largest tankers, making New Orleans an important center for the petrochemical industry. Always the lifeline of the city, "Ol' Man River" wouldn't be the same without its ubiquitous steamboats, a colorful reminder of the days of the pioneers.

The French Quarter (these pages and overleaf) is the familiar face of the old city, its streets bustling with activity and alive with color. Royal Street (right and overleaf) dissects the Vieux Carré – the quarter's other name, meaning literally "old square" – and epitomizes its character. On either side of Jackson Square stand the Pontalba buildings (bottom right), twin structures built in 1850 by a baroness of that name, who was reputed to have inspected the roof herself – wearing pantaloons!

Streetcars (above and below right) have a charm all their own. Tennessee Williams himself once lived in the French Quarter, on the line that ran the streetcar he made the most famous of them all: the one named "Desire." The horse, man's enduring servant, still finds a full day's work in the Vieux Carré (these pages and overleaf). It is often his cousin the mule that gets to wear the shady hat, however, while standing quietly before the spirited bronze steed in Jackson Square (facing page).

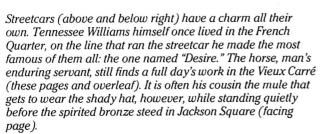

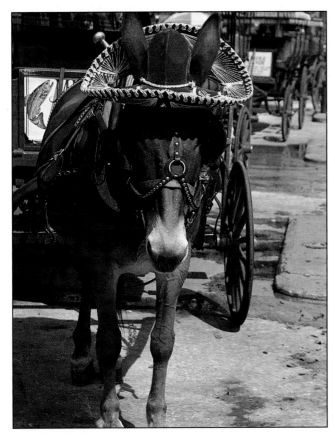

Nighttime in New Orleans offers something for everyone, and more. Welcoming bars and restaurants on Bourbon Street (facing page below) exude the old-time charm of the French Quarter (facing page top). Jazz music in various guises (above and right) drifts from every corner. The notorious red-light district (above right) caters for some tastes, while a hot dog seller (below) will satisfy others. Below right: the Jackson Brewery, and (overleaf) bright lights, big city.

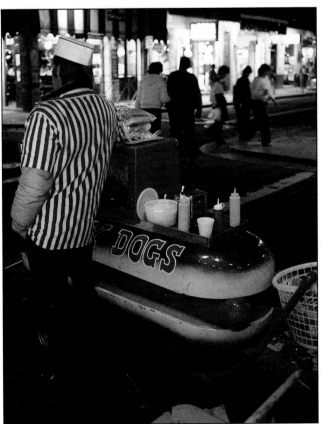

Jazz has been the spirit of New Orleans since the city was little more than a swamp in the early 1800s and the only music was that made by slaves beating drums and calabashes. The arrival of the French and the Spanish with their own distinctive musical heritage spawned a hybrid with African roots that was christened "jazz" somewhere along the way. The Preservation Hall (above, below and overleaf) and the Maison Bourbon (remaining pictures) are two New Orleans clubs that keep the tradition going.

The people of New Orleans (these pages) enjoy their city. Around any corner of the French Quarter, at any time of day, some kind of street entertainment can be found. Music, of course, is in the blood of the native New Orlean, as is the desire to share it – whether in a nightclub or on the sidewalk. Overleaf: Jackson Square.

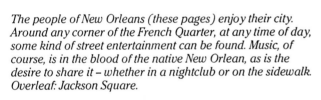

Mardi Gras, literally "Fat Tuesday," marks the last day before Lent, upon which it is traditional to indulge in excesses. Nothing if not excessive, the celebrations in New Orleans constitute a jamboree (these pages and overleaf) that is possibly unrivaled in all Christendom. The origin of the parade and its traditions is a subject for debate. Some say the hurling of trinkets from the floats was inspired by the gesture of a noblewoman way back when, who, finding her pearls restrictive, threw them into the assembled crowd.

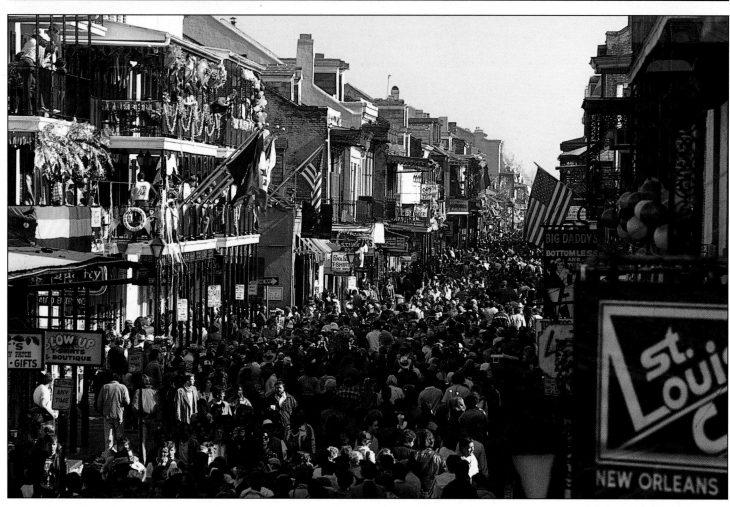

42

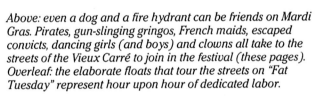

Above: even a dog and a fire hydrant can be friends on Mardi Gras. Pirates, gun-slinging gringos, French maids, escaped convicts, dancing girls (and boys) and clowns all take to the streets of the Vieux Carré to join in the festival (these pages). Overleaf: the elaborate floats that tour the streets on "Fat Tuesday" represent hour upon hour of dedicated labor.

The walls of the colorful dwellings in the French Quarter *(these pages)* radiate the atmosphere of the olden days, when *Jean Lafitte sent sparks flying in his blacksmith's shop (below left) on Bourbon Street (left). The romantic jumble of iron, timber, brick and plaster forms an architectural montage that is at once linear in style yet flamboyant in detail. Facing page: quaint galleries and antique shops on Chartres Street.*

46

The architecture in New Orleans (these pages) is second to that of no other American city. Intricate ironwork balconies, gates and railings form lace collars on the handsome old buildings in the Vieux Carré. The LaBrance Building (facing page top) on Royal Street is a particularly fine example, its filigree ironwork cast in an acorn and oak-leaf design. Tulane University (right) and the Cabildo (facing page bottom) are also jewels in the crown of the city. Above right: Saint Louis Cathedral, and (overleaf) the stern-wheeler Natchez.

Color, form and space were all carefully considered in the design of the modern Riverwalk development (above left, below and overleaf). Another innovative open-air complex is the Piazza d'Italia (left and facing page) by Charles Moore, with its imaginative mix of the classical and the up-to-the-minute. Above: the World Trade Center and the Joan of Arc statue. Below left: the Natchez, an exact replica of the type of stern-wheeler that would have plied the waters of "Ol' Man River" 200 years ago.

The historic houses in and around New Orleans stand out as prime examples of the tradition of Grand Homes of the South. San Francisco (facing page bottom and below), near Reserve, and Oak Alley (facing page top, above left and overleaf), near Vacherie, are plantation houses of palatial proportions that are open to the public. The decorous rooms of Hermann-Grima House (above and below left) on St. Louis Street are also open to view. The Steamboat House (left), built in 1875 by Milton P. Doullut, is one of a pair near the Mississippi.

The settlers way down south in the swamplands had a hard time building the city that became New Orleans. Man may have tamed the waters of the Misssissippi enough to venture upon them in light craft (facing page bottom) as well as in the robust stern-wheelers (overleaf) of old, but the swamps (facing page top) remain. Below and last page: Saint Louis Cathedral, Jackson Square.